Best Friends

© 2015 by Melissa Henry Stover. All rights reserved.

No part of this book may be reproduced in any written, electronic, recording, or photocopying without written permission of the publisher or author. The exception would be in the case of brief quotations embodied in the critical articles or reviews and pages where permission is specifically granted by the publisher or author.

Although every precaution has been taken to verify the accuracy of the information contained herein, the author and publisher assume no responsibility for any errors or omissions. No liability is assumed for damages that may result from the use of information contained within.

Gyfted Ink LLC

Books may be purchased by contacting the publisher and author at:

gyftedink@gmail.com

Publisher: Gyfted Ink, a division of Gyfted Ink, LLC

Editor: Melissa Henry Stover

Creative Consultant: To God be the glory

Library of Congress Catalog Number: 2015907143

{Gyfted Ink LLC} {Lugoff, SC}

ISBN-13: 978-0692435434 (Gyfted Ink)

ISBN-10: 0692435433

1. Action 2. Suspense

First Edition

Printed in United States

Best Friends

BEST FRIENDS

MELISSA HENRY STOVER

Best Friends

CHAPTER 1

Graduation day was upon them and pretty soon they would be separated for the first time that either one of the girls could remember. Tracy and Carmen had been best friends since first grade. They came from two totally different worlds. Tracy born into the home of a Baptist preacher raised her to be kind, caring, giving, and God fearing. While Carmen on the other hand took her first drink at age three from one of her mother's many different boyfriends. These two girls were like night and day. But nothing could break the bond of friendship that they had grown over the years until now.

Tracy was very excited about going off to New York. She would be attending Columbia. Carmen would be staying in town to attend a two year school. She could not afford a four year college, so she had to accept the two year scholarship instead. Carmen was sad, because over the years she had shared so much with Tracy. But she never told Tracy how her mother's boyfriends had introduced her to sex at an early age. How her mother sold her off to pay off her drug debt. Or how her mother would beat her if she tried to resist the men. Carmen carried a secret for two years that she told no one. She was in love with Tracy. She wanted to spend the rest of her life with Tracy, but had told no one for fear of rejection and losing Tracy altogether. So she kept quiet and cherished all the moments that they shared as best friends. People talked, so Tracy had heard rumors about the life that her best friend had. Never once did she ask Carmen, because she wanted Carmen to feel at peace with at least one person in this world.

Best Friends

As the sun beat down on the football field, no one seemed to mind the heat. Graduation day, they had finally made it. As Tracy looked at her best friend Carmen, she was so proud of her. After all she had been through, she managed to graduate high school. Her whole life had been a living hell. Except for the time she spent with Tracy. She had sworn off men long before Tracy ever started thinking about them. After graduation the girls celebrated with Tracy's parents, seeing as Carmen's mother was too wasted to even stay for the whole ceremony. After dinner Tracy's parents gave her a brand new car. They were proud of their daughter and wanted her to know how much they loved her .This way she could come home as often as she liked. Just when they thought that things couldn't get any better Tracy's dad pulled a car exactly like it out of the garage and handed Carmen the keys. Over the years they had come to love her as if she were one of their own and wanted her to know that they loved her too. As Carmen drifted off to sleep that night, she dreamed of her and Tracy living in a nice little house with their matching cars out front. She couldn't wait for that day to tell Tracy how much she loved her. Then the one person that she truly loved would belong to her and only her. About a week before Tracy was leaving for New York, she and Carmen decided to go to a party given by one of their former classmates. It seemed like a good idea.

CHAPTER 2

As soon as they arrived, Jeff Wilson the class jock asked Tracy to dance. She accepted, seeing as she had an enormous crush on him. Carmen couldn't stand to see his hands on Tracy. She felt as if she was losing control. She bit her lip until it bled, and the moment the dance was over with she told Tracy she wasn't feeling well and was ready to leave. On the way home Tracy told Carmen how cute she thought Jeff was and how giddy she felt in his arms. Carmen barely heard the words over the rage she felt in her head. She wanted to scream. Then Tracy dropped a bomb on her that Jeff would also be going to Columbia. He had asked Tracy if they could go out sometimes at school. Tracy was so excited that she didn't even noticed the look of pure rage in Carmen's eyes. Carmen had to figure out a way to keep Jeff from Tracy. Tracy belonged to her and she would do anything to keep her anything. That night as she drifted off to sleep she smiled.

Jeff would never get his hands on Tracy and she knew exactly what needed to be done. As the alarm went off at 4a.m. Carmen jumped up. She didn't want to wake her mother if that was possible, considering all the empty bottles that lay scattered across the floor. She carefully stepped over her half-dressed mother and her totally naked boyfriend to get to the door.

The morning air was cool on her face as she walked across town. She crossed the road and hid in the bushes and waited for Jeff's father to leave for work. Jeff's car was parked by the garage so she began to put her plan in motion. At least one of her mother's boyfriends was good for something. She had this one guy who would take her to his car repair shop to have sex with her and after they were finished he would show her how to repair cars as if nothing ever happened. She checked to make sure no one was looking than she carefully slid under the car and cut his brake line. No one would notice the spill because of the grass and she made sure to make it look like a break instead of a cut, so they would think that Jeff just had a terrible accident. She laughed at the thought of old Jeff trying to mash the brakes. This was the beginning of a new life for her and Tracy. Jeff was just a casualty of war. As she slid back

into her bed she whispered,
"Best friends are forever."

CHAPTER 3

As Tracy settled into to college life, she began to meet new people. She still hadn't completely gotten over Jeff's death. He was on his way to meet some friends before heading off to school and ran off of a cliff. They said that it was just a freak accident that maybe Jeff had swerved to avoid something and lost control. It was hard first semester, but Tracy threw herself into her work. Talking to her parents and Carmen always made her feel better. The first year seemed to fly by and summer was two weeks away. Tracy shared an apartment with two other girls and they asked Tracy to go skiing with them, she agreed. As she told Carmen of how she would be spending the first two weeks of her summer Carmen began to cry. Tracy laughed and that made Carmen furious. Tracy told Carmen that they both had to move on with their lives but they would always be best friends. It took every ounce of strength

Carmen had to wait those two weeks for Tracy, but the homecoming wasn't what she expected at all. As Tracy pulled into the yard Carmen noticed another car right behind her.

As Carmen went to meet Tracy, the guy in the car beat her to it. Carmen watched in total disgust as Tracy wrapped her arms around him and kissed him softly on the lips. Carmen could feel her blood boil, and she saw red. Tracy thought that she would surprise everyone by bringing home her new boyfriend Dave. They had been dating all year, but Tracy didn't tell anyone for fear that things wouldn't work out. But she announced to everyone that she and Dave were serious. Dave had proposed, and she accepted on the condition that they both finish college first. With that statement her father let out a sigh of relief and everyone laughed except for Carmen.

Best Friends

CHAPTER 4

At home Carmen took a butcher's knife and stabbed a stuffed animal that Tracy had given her just before leaving for college. "How could she do this to me? After all we've been through." said Carmen stabbing the stuffed animal until it was just stuffing. She had to figure out a way to get rid of him. No one would have Tracy, except her no one. Jeff got in her way and she got rid of him, and now Dave would pay the price also. The next day they all went on a picnic. Carmen could barely contain her emotions as Dave held Tracy's hand. Inside her head she was screaming "don't touch her she's mine! "Every time they kissed she winced with pain. They began to talk about growing up, and all the fun they had as kids. They talked about parachuting with Tracy's dad and her brother Rob.

That's when it hit Carmen she had the perfect way to get rid of Dave. She suggested that they all go parachuting. All the old equipment was in the garage, and Dave could use Rob's gear since he was away studying in Europe.

Best Friends

CHAPTER 5

Dave had never been parachuting before so was a bit reluctant until Tracy affectionately convinced him to go. Carmen almost lost her lunch, but knowing that Dave would soon be out of their lives gave her the strength to keep it down. Carmen suggested that she stay the night, so they could all get an early start the next morning. As everyone slept, Carmen snuck out to the garage. She used a flashlight to keep from turning on the lights. She found Rob's parachute bag and got to work. She cut holes in the parachute, not enough to look suspicious, but enough to do the trick. As she lay on the couch and drifted off to sleep she whispered "Best friends are forever." She held her pillow tight and imagined Tracy in her arms. After tomorrow Dave would be out of their lives forever. Carmen had the best night sleep since Tracy arrived home with Dave. She awoke

feeling refreshed and ready to
go.

As they headed out Tracy's parents warned them to be careful. They wouldn't be going they wanted the kids to have some fun. They enjoyed having some time alone too. The house had been so busy since Tracy came home. As they drove off Tracy's father said "Oh gosh I meant to check the backpacks before they left. Tracy mom said, "I'm sure everything's okay. Honey, you worry too much!" "Guess I do." Tracy's father answered.

CHAPTER 6

As the plane roared Dave tried one last time to back out. Tracy promised him that everything would be okay, and when they reached down that she would give him a big kiss. She reminded him of their special plans for the night. They were going to spend the evening at her parent's cottage, just the two of them. That's what you think screamed Carmen in her head!"

They decided that Dave should go second. Maybe seeing Tracy jump would put him at ease. Just before Tracy jumped she leaned over and kissed Dave and said "I love you." And then she was gone. Dave turned to Carmen who was staring at him with cold eyes. When she realized he was looking at her she put on her best smile and said "Your turn. Just remember everything we told you and you'll be just fine."

Best Friends

Dave jumped and Carmen laughed as she jumped behind him. As the air meet her face Carmen grinned that devilish grin and gave herself up to the sky. She noticed Tracy pulling her cord and knew that Dave's fate was only moments away. She felt as if she owned the world.

As Dave began to pull his cord Carmen whisked by him and smiled. Dave felt a strange sense of panic. Tracy was below and saw none of what was going on. Carmen never once looked up. She kept her eyes on the prize Tracy. As Dave flew past her screaming for help Carmen winked at him and pulled her cord. She went up and Dave went down. He went past Tracy so fast she didn't realize what was going on until it was too late. As Dave frantically fell to earth

Tracy began to cry, and Carmen began to laugh.

CHAPTER 7

Best Friends

Tracy stayed home first semester of the second year. She could not face going back to New York without Dave. She was beginning to wonder if God was playing a cruel trick on her. First Jeff and now Dave. She didn't know how much more of this she could take. Her father reminded her that God would not put more on her than she could bear. He told her to look to God and he would give her strength. She knew her father was right but her faith was slowly slipping away.

Tracy and Carmen spent a lot of time together over the next couple of months. Their friendship grew and Carmen's obsession for Tracy grew more haunting with each passing day. As they were having dinner at Tracy's house one night Tracy announced that she was ready to return to school. Tracy's father saw the look of distress on Carmen's face.

He told Tracy that he was proud of her, and that he thought it was time for her to move on with her life. He couldn't shake the feeling that something was wrong with Carmen, but he let it slide. The more Tracy talked of her plans to return to school, the more Carmen withdrew from the conversation. She could not stand the thought of losing Tracy again. Tracy once more threw herself into her work. She didn't go out she only studied. She promised herself that she would never fall in love again. That was music to Carmen's ears. She spent her time studying and daydreaming about Tracy. She often visited Tracy's parents at their Pet shop. She would be so happy when she would talk about Tracy. Her father became worried.

Best Friends

CHAPTER 8

He felt that Carmen was too attached to Tracy. He suggested that maybe Tracy should stay in New York for the summer, to keep her mind off of what happened at home the summer before. His suspicions were verified when he saw the look on Carmen's face when he gave her the news.

Tracy would come home for two weeks and then head back to New York for the rest of the summer. Tracy's father suggested to Carmen that maybe she should date. He told her that even though Tracy was her best friend that she should consider her future. Hopefully Tracy will soon get married and move away. You have to face the facts that you and Tracy will never be together like the old days. So take my advice and move on.

Best Friends

Carmen just looked at him and said "I don't want to move on. She's my best friend and best friends are forever. With that statement Carmen left the pet shop, and vowed that no one would keep her from Tracy not even her father.

That night Carmen contemplated her ultimate plan. She knew that Tracy's Father would get in the way, so she had to get rid of him. How could she possibly get rid of him without drawing suspicion? As she lay in bed her mind went to work and Carmen knew exactly what she needed to do.

The next day she called Tracy to see when she would be coming home. Tracy told her that she would be coming home in a week. That her mother was coming to visit and would be making the trip with her. That was perfect Carmen thought. Now all I have to do is wait. She smiled as she went to sleep, thinking of finally having Tracy without anyone stopping them. She would finally have Tracy all to herself.

The next morning as Tracy's father got out of his car to open the shop, he got a call on his cellphone. It was Carmen she said that Tracy had tried to reach him at home, but he was already gone, and she couldn't get through on his cellphone. Tracy had broken down on her way home and needed him to come pick her and her mother up. She told him the directions and also told him that Tracy said she would not have her phone on it was running weak and it had to be recharged.

Best Friends

CHAPTER 9

Carmen also asked him if she could go. He said "Yes". Carmen was already about forty miles out of town she told him she had gotten a head start just in case she couldn't reach him. She told him that she would meet him at a park in the next town over and leave her car.

As Tracy's father pulled up he noticed the door to Carmen's car was open, but there was no one inside. He proceeded to the car and found that no one was inside. As he was about to turn around, he felt a sharp pain in his back. As he turned around there stood Carmen stabbing him over and over again. She began to yell, "YOU WILL NOT KEEP ME FROM TRACY SHE IS MINE AND I LOVE HER!" He tried to fight her off, but he couldn't. Before his world turned black the last memory he had was Carmen standing over him smiling.

As Tracy and her mother
came into town they thought
that it was odd that the store
was closed. So they decided to
go home. They thought that
maybe her dad was planning a
surprise for them. As they pulled
into the yard they noticed that
his truck was not there and
began to worry. They called
everyone they could think of and
no one had seen him including
Carmen. She came right over as
soon as she knew they were
home. Secretly she smiled

knowing that now no one could keep her from Tracy. Just as they were about to call the police the phone rang. Tracy listened intently and hung up the phone.

As she turned around her mother knew that something was terribly wrong. Tracy braced herself before telling her mother that her father had been brutally attacked. Her mother began to demand answers, but Tracy had none. She told her Mother that the Sheriff would be out to talk to them soon. Carmen inwardly smiled, because she had all the answers they needed, or so she thought. A few minutes later the police arrived Carmen never blinked as the police approached the house, they asked which one was Tracy. Tracy identified herself as soon as she did the officers grabbed Carmen and handcuffed her. Everyone began screaming, no one knew what was going on.

Best Friends

CHAPTER 10

Best Friends

We got to go to the hospital now", said Tracy. As they arrived to the hospital they were greeted by a doctor. "I'm sorry to be the one to tell you this but your father in a coma. I'm afraid I don't know when or if he will awake" the doctor reported. .

"There must be some mistake Carmen would never attack my dad," Tracy said started crying. Two weeks went back still no change but Tracy's mom refused to leave his side.

Finally Tracy's mom went downstairs to get some coffee. Tracy's father's hand began to move. Than he opened his eyes. "Do you know what happen?" Tracy asked. Hoping he remembered what happened. "Yes I was attacked," her father answered. "We know you was attacked" Tracy responded. "But who?" "It was Carmen",

Best Friends

The last thing she heard Carmen yell was "BEST FRIENDS ARE FOREVER". That phrase rung in her mind over the next several months.

Best Friends

CHAPTER 11

Best Friends

It was a slow road to recovery for her father but with lots of love and therapy, he was able to attend Carmen's trial to testify against her. Carmen wrote Tracy every day, telling her how much she loved her and how glad she was that everyone knew. She told Tracy how she dreamt of spending the rest of her life with her. Tracy was totally devastated. She never knew that her best friend had fallen in love with her. She never wrote Carmen back. Sometimes she didn't even open the letters this was not the Carmen she knew and she refused to believe that Carmen was in her right mind.

She talked her father into agreeing to have Carmen committed for three years instead of arrested. They loved Carmen and felt that she needed therapy instead of jail. At the trial Tracy never looked at Carmen. This made Carmen angry after all she did for her, and to be with her how she could just ignore her. She vowed that Tracy would still be hers one day.

It had been three years since Tracy had been home and it would probably be another thirty before she would even consider going back. So many bad things had happened there for her that she decided to never go back and started over. She was now a successful lawyer in a prestigious law firm. She was married to a wonderful man. He was a doctor and he loved Tracy with all of his heart. Tracy met Todd when she returned to New York after the trial. She had begun to see a therapist to help deal with all the trauma in her life. Todd's office was next door to her therapist. One day as she was on her way to her appointment she broke her heel and fell. As she struggled to get up, a strong hand reached down and picked her up. As she looked into Todd's eyes her heart skipped a beat. And they haven't been apart since. She loves telling anyone who will listen about how Todd literally swept her off her feet.

She kept nothing from Todd, so he knew all about Carmen and her Past track record with men she liked and loved. Todd promised Tracy that he wouldn't die on her or leave her. Tracy felt at peace with Todd she hardly ever thought of her past.

Best Friends

CHAPTER 12

Her parents came to visit regularly, and that's all she needed from home. Her mother seemed very nervous this visit and Tracy wanted to know why, her mother finally broke down and told her that Carmen had been released from the mental hospital earlier in the week. Tracy assured her mother that there was nothing to worry about. Carmen has had all the help she needed.

Tracy had taken a leave of absence from work. Carmen had followed Tracy's parents and was sitting outside of her house watching her and her mother talk. It felt so good to see Tracy again. Carmen had waited three years to see the love of her life and it was worth the wait. She knew that she had to be careful. She would be patient this time. She would do whatever it took to be in Tracy's life whatever. She stayed there and watched Tracy all evening. She wasn't mad at

Tracy for not waiting for her, or not writing her she loved her and would forgive her of anything. For Todd things were quite different. She vowed to get him away from Tracy one way or the other.

As Tracy and her family went on with their lives, Carmen began planning her strategy for getting rid of Todd and getting Tracy back for good this time. She began following Todd and tracking his every move. She knew what time he got up, what time he left home, and even what time he went to lunch every day. She started out her plan very slowly. She began calling the house when Tracy was home alone. She would say nothing and just hang up. She decided to place some doubt in Tracy's mind about her perfect marriage. She would call at 2am at 4 am and then again at 6. Tracy didn't know what to think.

Things at her job were going great. She was being looked at to become a senior partner it was between her and Jennifer Wilcox. They both were great attorneys and Tracy knew that she might not get the job. Little did Tracy know that Carmen had taken a job in the mail room under a false name and was watching her every move. She also knew that Jennifer would probably get the job. She had to do something she could not let Tracy be looked over for this job .She would do

anything for her, anything. That
night Jennifer worked late she
was doing everything she could
to impress the senior partners.
As she stepped out of the
elevator she felt as if someone
was watching her.as she turned
to stick the key in her door,
Carmen appeared out of
nowhere. She had a knife and
told Jennifer not to scream.
Jennifer begged her to take her
money and her car, but Carmen
just laughed. She told Jennifer
that there was no way that she

would stand around and watch her take that job from Tracy. Jennifer begged and pleaded with Carmen to let her go. So Carmen backed off and told Jennifer to go home. Jennifer smiled as she slid her key into the locked at that very moment she felt the knife as it slid into her flesh. Carmen stood over her as she took her last breath and whispered "best friends are forever".

Best Friends

CHAPTER 13

The next morning it was all over the news about Jennifer's death. As Tracy and Todd watched the news there was a knock at the door. It was the police. They had a search warrant, and advised Todd of his rights. Tracy and Todd were devastated, they had no idea what was going on. They asked Todd if he had an alibi for ten o'clock the previous night and he said no he was home alone and Tracy was at a late dinner meeting with some clients. Just then another officer appeared in the kitchen holding a bloody knife. Tracy and Todd were both shocked. The police told Todd that they also found his watch at the murder scene. The detective stated that they found the knife hidden under some oil rags in the garage. The knife came from a set of knives in their kitchen that they hardly ever used.

Tracy watched as they took Todd away. Her whole world was crumbling right before her very eyes. She didn't know what to believe. Could the man she slept beside every night be capable of murder? Yes she wanted the job badly, but never bad enough to take someone's life for it. Tracy felt a strange feeling come over her it's the same feeling she had gotten when Jeff, and Dave had died. God what could I have possibly done wrong to deserve this? Tracy wanted to believe

Todd when he said that he didn't kill Jennifer, but the evidence was overwhelming.

She paced the floor all day long trying to figure out what happened. She spent the night praying that God would help her through the days to come. At that very moment the phone rang. Tracy listened very carefully and she hung up. As the investigator was talking to Tracy walked out to her mailbox and inside was a large brown envelope. Inside she found the investigator's report and the pictures of Carmen killing

Jennifer and sneaking into their house.

CHAPTER 14

Carmen awoke that very same morning, as if she had not murdered someone in cold blood the night before. She turned on the news and listened as they described Jennifer's as if it was the weather report. She laughed as she thought of how she carefully got rid of Todd and Jennifer at the same time. She knew that sneaking into the house that night would be hard, but it had been worth the risk. As Todd lay asleep on the couch she had climbed up on the bedroom balcony and snuck in and removed the watch. After she killed Jennifer she snuck into the garage and hid the knife. Her plan could not have went any better.

Just as she was about to pour herself a cup of coffee the doorbell rang. At the door was a man she had never met before. He introduced himself as Dan Bigley. She told him she was not interested. That's when he held up a picture of her climbing the balcony at Tracy's last night.

She decided to invite him in. He explained to her that Tracy had hired him several weeks ago to see if her husband was cheating on her. He told her how he noticed her watching the house as well as him. He decided not to mention her to Tracy until he had some solid evidence. He told her how he had followed her the night before and chronicled her every move. He told Carmen that for one hundred thousand dollars he would turn over the pictures and the negatives to her and walk away. Carmen knew that she had to think quickly. She told him that she didn't have the money right then and that she had to go to work. She asked if she could meet him that night. He agreed to meet her at his office at 9o'clock. She promised not to be late.

She arrived fifteen minutes early. She told him that he would pay for deceiving her. He begged for his life but Carmen shot him twice in the chest. She yelled that she killed Jeff, she killed Dave, she killed Jennifer, and now she had killed him. She screamed that it was all his fault. She yelled that now she must kill Tracy and kill herself too. It was the only way that they could be together. She laughed and closed the door. Thinking that she had once again gotten away with murder. Now she had the evidence and the money the only thing she didn't have was Tracy.

CHAPTER 15

As Tracy tried to decide what to do her phone rang once again. The call was to tell her the plan to catch Carmen and put her away for life. As she listened very carefully a smile came upon her face, but at that very same moment she felt the cold barrel of a gun against her face. She screamed and dropped the phone. After all these years she was staring Carmen in the face. Carmen looked like a wild beast. She grabbed Tracy and hugged her. Tracy could not stand her touch.

She began to tell Tracy of how they could run away together and no one could find them. Tracy began to tell her no and Carmen went crazy. "After all I've done for us." "What are you talking about?" Tracy asked?

Carmen began to tell Tracy everything from the beginning.

Tracy stood frozen in horror as Carmen told her of how she killed Jeff, Dave, tried to kill her father, then Jennifer, and the investigator Tracy had hired. Tracy watched as Carmen bragged about all of this as if she had won a gold medal. At that moment Tracy bolted for the balcony, and Carmen came chasing. She grabbed Tracy and threw her into the railing. "You are ungrateful, after all I've done for you." Carmen yelled, Tracy began to cry. Don't cry Carmen whispered as she stroked Tracy's face. I promise we will never be apart again. No one will keep me from you. She helped Tracy up. The private investigator and the police kick in Tracy's door. She didn't realize they were also watching the house. Carmen's smile faded away.

Best Friends

Tracy knew this would be her last chance to fight for her life. Tracy knocked the gun from Carmen's hand. They began to struggle and Carmen went over the balcony. Tracy grabbed her hand and tried to hold on. Tracy told Carmen to forget about her and let her move on with her life. She had found happiness in her life with Todd. She then looked up at Tracy who was losing her grip. She smiled and said "You won't let me fall we're best friends and best friends are forever. The sirens were growing closer. Tracy took one last look at her friend and said "With best friends like you who needs enemies." With that she let go and walked away.

Tracy turn the evidence over to the police and Todd was later released. With Carmen gone they had nothing to fear.

www.ingramcontent.com/pod-product-compliance
Lightning Source LLC
Chambersburg PA
CBHW081154090426
42736CB00017B/3324